LITTLE LIBRARY NUMBER ONE

GRANUAILE

JOHN & FATTI BURKE

GILL BOOKS

**Y**oung Gráinne O'Malley wanted to be a great sailor and leader. She and her parents lived near Clew Bay in County Mayo.

Her father was a merchant with many ships. He took her sailing and fishing, and taught her about the tides and the weather.

Teenage Gráinne was expected to be a lady and marry a chieftain, but she wanted to go to sea and have adventures.

Everyone said that sailing was for boys only, but Gráinne knew that was just silly.

One day she heard that a ship was going to Spain to sell hides and buy wine. Gráinne wanted to go. Her parents said, 'No, it's too dangerous. Your beautiful long hair will get caught in the rigging and we might lose you.' But Gráinne had a solution.

She cut off her hair and dressed in sailor's clothes. With her hair short, she was called 'Granuaile' or 'Bald Gráinne'. And so her parents agreed to let her sail to Spain.

The sailors on the ship were merchants, but they were also pirates! So Granuaile became a sailor on her father's ship, and sometimes robbed other ships, too.

Very soon, the other sailors said
that she was as good as them.
But Granuaile knew she
was better.

On their way back from Spain, the ship was attacked! Gráinne was told to go below and hide, but instead she climbed up the mast.

There she spotted a pirate about to kill her father, so she bravely jumped down onto the pirate's back and saved her father's life. The crew drove off the enemy and cheered for Granuaile.

Later, Granuaile met Dónal O'Flaherty, a Galway chieftain's son. They loved each other and were married and had three children, Eóghan, Maeve and Murrough.

Dónal was always fighting for more land and power, and so was known as 'Dónal of the Battles'. He died while fighting with the Joyce Clan. The Clan tried to take over Dónal's castle but Granuaile drove them away.

Dónal's family, the O'Flaherty Clan, would not let Granuaile be their new leader. So she went back to Mayo with her children, her sailors and her ships, and became leader of the O'Malley clan instead.

O'MALLEY CLAN

JOYCE CLAN

With castles all along the west coast of Ireland, Granuaile ruled the seas and islands. She became known as 'The Pirate Queen'.

The Pirate Queen had many adventures. One night, during a terrible storm, she heard about a shipwreck. Risking her life on the wild ocean, she bravely rescued Hugh de Lacy, a young man from Wexford.

Another time, Granuaile was sailing
down the east coast and stopped at
Howth Castle for a rest. But the gates
were locked and she was told to go
away because the family were having
their dinner.

Fiery Granuaile saw the Lord's grandson playing outside and kidnapped him! She said she would return the child if the Lord promised never to lock the gates of Howth Castle and to always set an extra place at the table. He agreed and his grandson was returned home safe and sound.

After several years,
Granuaile married again.
Her husband was Richard-
in-Iron Bourke. Their son,
Tibbot, was born at sea!

Algerian pirates attacked
Granuaile's ship and came on
board. After giving birth to Tibbot,
Granuaile rushed out of her cabin
to help her crew defeat the pirates.

She returned home with not just
a captured ship, but a new baby
as well!

Richard Bingham, the English governor of Connacht, was Granuaile's greatest enemy. He arrested her sons Murrough and Tibbot, and this made Granuaile furious! So she sailed to England to meet Queen Elizabeth and make a deal. Granuaile did not speak English and the Queen had no Irish, so they spoke to each other in Latin.

Queen Elizabeth agreed to release her sons and move Richard Bingham out of Ireland. In return, Granuaile promised to stop attacking English ships.

But years later, Queen Elizabeth sent Bingham back to Ireland, so Granuaile went back to her old ways, too.

She remained a fearless leader of both land and sea, the Pirate Queen of Mayo.

Timeline

1530
Gráinne is born
in County Mayo

1546
Marries Dónal an
Chogaidh O'Flaherty

1560
Dónal is
killed in battle

1564
Gráinne returns to
Mayo and settles on
Clare Island, where
she becomes the
Pirate Queen

1566
Marries
Richard-in-Iron
Bourke

1565
Rescues Hugh de Lacy
from a shipwreck

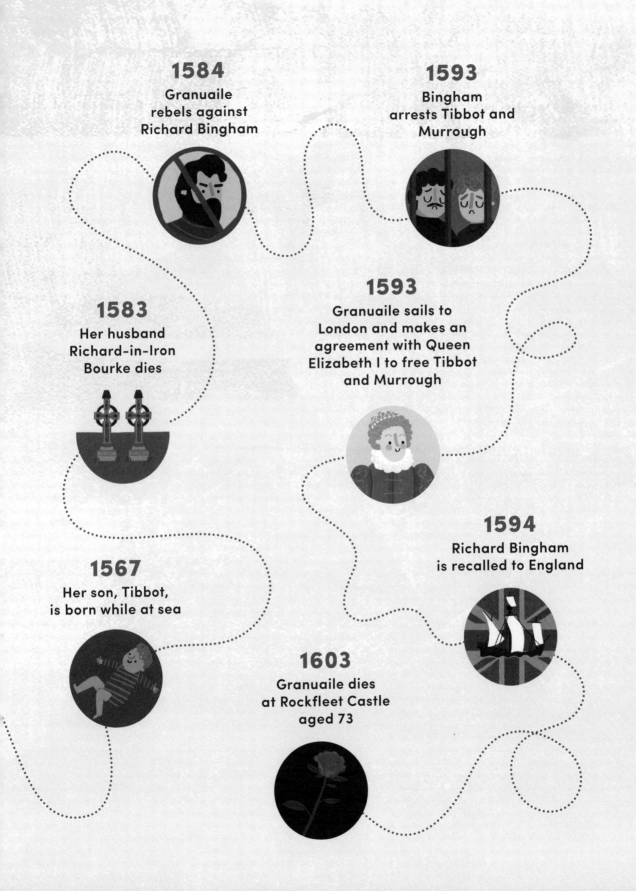

1584
Granuaile rebels against Richard Bingham

1593
Bingham arrests Tibbot and Murrough

1583
Her husband Richard-in-Iron Bourke dies

1593
Granuaile sails to London and makes an agreement with Queen Elizabeth I to free Tibbot and Murrough

1567
Her son, Tibbot, is born while at sea

1594
Richard Bingham is recalled to England

1603
Granuaile dies at Rockfleet Castle aged 73

Did You Know?

The castle that Granuaile defended against the Joyce clan is now called HEN'S CASTLE.

Granuaile's son, Tibbott, was knighted after her death and became VISCOUNT MAYO.

There is still an EMPTY PLACE set at the dining table in Howth Castle to this day!

Granuaile was an only child but she had a half-brother, the son of her father, called DÓNAL NA PÍOPA (Donal of the Pipes).

In 1578 a PRICE OF £200 was offered for the capture of Granuaile. This would be worth over €100,000 in today's money!

She was very close to her daughter, Maeve. Maeve married another Richard Bourke, known as 'THE DEVIL'S HOOK'.

Granuaile became LADY BOURKE in 1581 when her husband, Richard, was knighted.

Nicknames were very common in Ireland. Tibbott was known as 'Tibbott na Long' meaning 'TIBBOTT OF THE SHIPS'.

It is said that when visiting Queen Elizabeth I, Granuaile was offered a handkerchief to blow her nose. When she had used it, she THREW IT INTO THE FIRE. This shocked those present because the lace handkerchief was very expensive.

The Commissioners of Irish Lights vessel is called the ILV GRANUAILE.

The original WESTPORT HOUSE in Mayo was built on the site of an O'Malley Castle by Colonel John Browne and his wife Maud Bourke. Maud Bourke was Granuaile's great-granddaughter.

There is a STATUE OF GRANUAILE outside Westport House in County Mayo.

You can visit CLARE ISLAND, home to Granuaile, by taking the ferry from Roonagh Quay (west of Louisburgh). The journey takes just 10 minutes.

There are many WONDERFUL THINGS to do on Clare Island, such as snorkelling, rock-climbing, raft-building, biking and coasteering.

You can also take boat trips around CLEW BAY and see the other islands that Granuaile knew so well.

ABOUT the AUTHORS

KATHI 'FATTI' BURKE is an Irish illustrator. She lives in Amsterdam.

JOHN BURKE is Fatti's dad. He is a retired primary school teacher and principal. He lives in Waterford.

Their first book, *Irelandopedia*, won *The Ryan Tubridy Show* Listeners' Choice Award at the Irish Book Awards 2015, and the Eilís Dillon Award for first children's book and the Judges' Special Award at the CBI Book of the Year Awards 2016. Their next books, *Historopedia* and *Foclóiropedia*, were nominated for the Specsavers Children's Book of the Year (Junior) Award at the Irish Book Awards 2016 and 2017. Their books have sold over 100,000 copies in Ireland.

BY the SAME AUTHORS

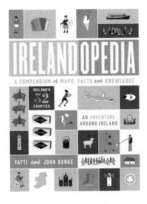

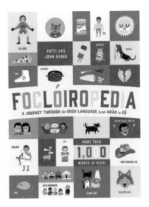

'One of the most
entertaining reference
books we have had for
some time'
THE IRISH TIMES

'The book that every
family needs to have in
their house'
RYAN TUBRIDY

'A perfect – and
educational – gift
for kids of all ages'
MUMMYPAGES.IE

Gill Books
Hume Avenue
Park West
Dublin 12
www.gillbooks.ie

Gill Books is an imprint of M.H. Gill and Co.

Text © John Burke 2018
Illustrations © Kathi Burke 2018
978 07171 8350 0

Designed by www.grahamthew.com
Printed by L&C Group, Poland
This book is typeset in 13pt on 25pt Sofia Pro.

A CIP catalogue record for this book is available
from the British Library.

5 4 3 2 1